Elizabeth

Written by
KATE WILLIAMS

Illustrated by
HELEN SHOESMITH

wren
&rook

Young Elizabeth

There was once a little girl called Elizabeth. But she wasn't just any little girl. She was a princess, and her grandparents were the king and queen of the United Kingdom!

Prince Albert and Princess Elizabeth celebrated the arrival of baby Elizabeth on 21 April 1926 in London. She was soon called "the world's best-known baby".

When her father and mother went to Australia and New Zealand on a royal visit, they were showered with *PRESENTS* for their daughter, and many children wrote her letters.

Four years later, Elizabeth became a big *SISTER* to Princess Margaret.

"Lilibet", as Elizabeth's family called her, was never meant to become queen. But over the years, lots of unexpected things happened.

When Elizabeth was nine, her **GRANDFATHER**, King George V, died and her Uncle Edward became king. But that winter, Elizabeth was writing up notes from her swimming lesson when she heard shouts outside. Her uncle Edward had given up the throne because he no longer wanted to be king!

This meant that Elizabeth's father was now king instead. Elizabeth rushed to tell Margaret, "When I'm older, I will be queen!"

Elizabeth's Uncle Edward stopped being king because he wished to marry a lady called Wallis Simpson. But Wallis had already been **MARRIED** before, and it was against the rules for a king to marry someone who had been divorced.

He chose **LOVE** over the crown!

War, weddings and new arrivals

Elizabeth may have been a princess, but like many other children her life changed when the Second World War began. It would be five long years.

In 1936, Elizabeth's father took the name King George VI. Then the **FAMILY** moved into Buckingham Palace.

When the **SECOND WORLD WAR** began in 1939, Elizabeth and Margaret were sent to Windsor Castle to keep them safe. When air-raid sirens rang, warning that bombs might be dropped, they hid in cold, beetle-infested dungeons!

Back in London, the bombs had destroyed parts of Buckingham Palace. The princesses' mother practised shooting a gun among the ruins in case of an **INVASION**!

To cheer everyone up, Elizabeth and Margaret would put on **PANTOMIMES** at Windsor Castle at Christmas. Prince Philip of Greece, who Elizabeth later married, would watch them.

Elizabeth wanted to help with the war effort. When she turned 18, she began training as a mechanic and ambulance driver to help injured soldiers.

On 8 May 1945, the war ended! Elizabeth and Margaret joined everyone **CELEBRATING** in the streets. They even joined in with a dance called the conga!

After the war, Elizabeth and Prince Philip fell in love. They had a large wedding and were married in Westminster Abbey in 1947.

Their first child, Prince Charles, was born a year later. They had four children in all: Prince Charles, Princess Anne, Prince Andrew and Prince Edward.

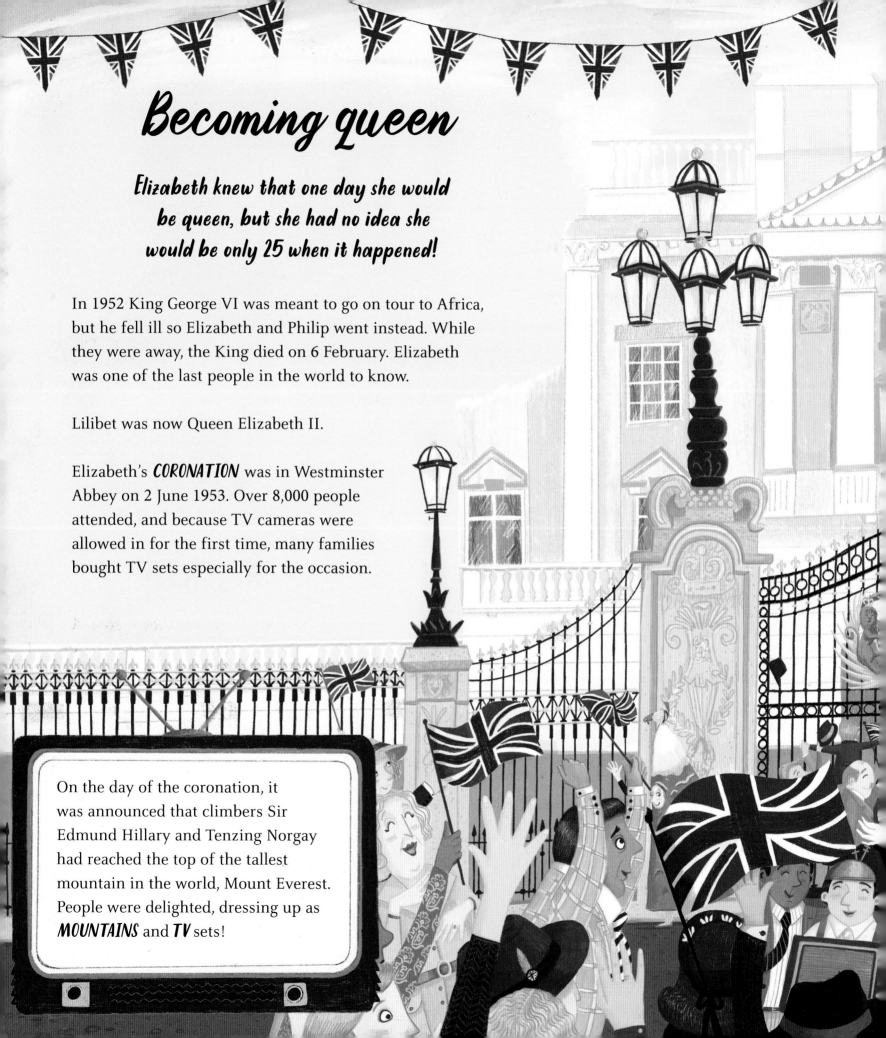

Becoming queen

Elizabeth knew that one day she would be queen, but she had no idea she would be only 25 when it happened!

In 1952 King George VI was meant to go on tour to Africa, but he fell ill so Elizabeth and Philip went instead. While they were away, the King died on 6 February. Elizabeth was one of the last people in the world to know.

Lilibet was now Queen Elizabeth II.

Elizabeth's **CORONATION** was in Westminster Abbey on 2 June 1953. Over 8,000 people attended, and because TV cameras were allowed in for the first time, many families bought TV sets especially for the occasion.

On the day of the coronation, it was announced that climbers Sir Edmund Hillary and Tenzing Norgay had reached the top of the tallest mountain in the world, Mount Everest. People were delighted, dressing up as **MOUNTAINS** and **TV** sets!

The coronation was shown around the **WORLD**. A special plane even flew the film recording to Canada. People there were able to watch the event the day it actually happened!

The duties of a queen

The Queen lives in a wonderful palace and has lots of beautiful corgis, horses and jewellery. But there are a lot of important things she has to do as well...

The Queen is the head of state of the United Kingdom and other countries including Australia and Barbados. This is known as the Commonwealth. The Queen represents these countries, but she does not rule them. That job is done by their governments.

The Queen has to **TRAVEL** lots to meet with **IMPORTANT** world leaders. If you add up all of the Queen's travels, she has been around the world over 40 times. Imagine all that packing!

In 1953 Elizabeth went on a Commonwealth tour on the royal yacht. She travelled 64,375 km by land, air and sea and visited places such as Australia and New Zealand. One of her favourite places is Canada – she has been there 27 times!

GREETINGS FROM Canada

Buckingham Palace,
Westminster,
LONDON,
United Kingdom
SW1A 1AA

Charles

Mummy x

Clarence House,
LONDON.
SW1A 1BA

NEW ZEALAND

Even though the Queen doesn't rule the United Kingdom, she still has to know what is going on. She has weekly updates with the **PRIME MINISTER**. She is not allowed to tell them what to do, but she does ask tough questions to keep them on their toes!

Her first prime minister was Winston Churchill, who led Britain during the Second World War. People always want to know who her favourite is, but the Queen will never tell who her favourite prime minister has been.

The Queen hosts many special dinners for kings, queens and rulers from other countries at Buckingham Palace.

On these occasions, the Palace uses a special dinner service made up of 4,000 items, including plates, dishes and cutlery. It is over **200 YEARS OLD**. It takes three weeks to unpack and polish and a very long time to wash up after dinner!

Each guest has a space of exactly 46 cm on the table. The Queen checks everything is perfect.

The biggest events in history

When the Queen was born, Britain and the world was very different. But over her lifetime, she has witnessed some of the biggest events and changes in history.

1900s

Countries that had once been controlled by the British Empire campaigned and fought to be **INDEPENDENT** and ruled by their own governments.

After they became independent, lots of countries came to work together as part of the **COMMONWEALTH**. There are 54 countries in the Commonwealth, and every four years they hold the Commonwealth Games – a big sports competition. The Games begin after the Queen presents a baton to a runner. The baton is then passed on by athletes around the world in a relay!

The **NATIONAL HEALTH SERVICE** was set up after the Second World War. Before this, many families could not afford to go to the doctor. But with the **NHS**, you can visit a doctor or hospital and you don't have to pay a penny for them to make you better again!

When the Queen came to the throne, lots of **FOOD** was unavailable because of the Second World War. But soon people could eat their favourite foods again and new ones were invented too. The first fish fingers were sold in **1955**, and we now eat 1.5 million a day!

1948

1955

1967

1950s and 1960s

After the Second World War, people from the Caribbean were invited to Britain to work. The first big group of people arrived in 1948 on a ship called **EMPIRE WINDRUSH**, with more following in the **1950s** and **1960s**. Many became key workers. They were often treated unfairly and sometimes cruelly due to the colour of their skin.

Norwell Roberts became the first black Metropolitan police officer in **1967**. He was born in Anguilla, in the Caribbean, and came to Britain when he was nine years old. He became a detective in the **1970s** and received a **MEDAL** from Prince Charles.

The swinging sixties was an **EXCITING** time when young people started wearing new fashions, such as the miniskirt, and listened to wildly popular bands such as The Beatles and The Rolling Stones.

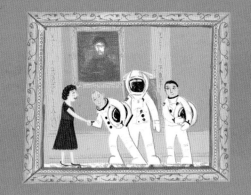

In **1969** people landed on the **MOON**. The Queen sent a message of congratulations to the astronauts, which is still on the Moon in a metal container today! The Queen invited the astronauts to Buckingham Palace (they all had bad colds at the time!). She was also visited by the first woman in space, Valentina Tereshkova, in **1964**.

1969

1968

In **1968** women working on sewing machines at the Ford car factory in Dagenham refused to do any more work until they were paid the same amount as men who did a similar job to them. Around the country, lots of women began to do the same. In 1970 a law was passed making sure women were paid the same as men.

In the **1970s** the price of oil started to go up, which meant electricity became more expensive. People were told they couldn't use as much electricity and often had to live by candlelight as power cuts became common.

Fashion started changing lots again too. Young people started dressing as **PUNKS** with spiky hair and ripped clothes!

1970s

1977

During the **1970s**, a huge plane called the "**JUMBO JET**" began taking passengers abroad. It was cheap to fly, so more people went on holiday. Food from other countries became popular too – such as pizza and pasta!

When the Queen was born, there were no home computers or mobile phones and the internet did not exist yet. The first home **COMPUTER** arrived in **1977** and children wanted one for Christmas so they could play games such as *Space Invaders*.

The Queen sent her first email in **1976** and her first Instagram post in **2019**.

The palaces

When the Queen isn't BUSY travelling around the world, she stays in one of her BIG, grand palaces.

The Queen has lots of palaces and residences. Buckingham Palace, Windsor Castle, Sandringham House and Balmoral Castle are the four best known.

Buckingham Palace has 775 rooms, including 52 bedrooms and 78 bathrooms. It has its own pool, home cinema, post office, police station and cash machine.

Buckingham Palace

Windsor Castle

Want to pop in to see the Queen? If the **ROYAL STANDARD** is flying, she's home. If you can see the Union Jack, she's out.

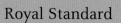

Royal Standard   Union Jack

The **LIMESTONE** rock used to build Buckingham Palace contains fossils that could be 200 million years old! And there is a network of secret tunnels underneath connecting the palace to local streets.

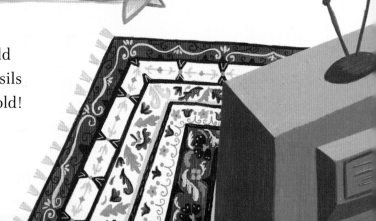

Sandringham House

Balmoral Castle

Sandringham is where the Queen celebrates **CHRISTMAS** every year and she goes to Balmoral Castle in Scotland each summer for a holiday. Queen Victoria bought Balmoral and covered it with tartan patterns because she loved Scotland so much.

The Queen also owns lots of interesting things. She keeps some in her houses, but the others are far too big or wild…

Property of the Queen

Lots of animals in the waters around the UK, including all the dolphins!

Most of the swans in the UK.

Two pieces of burnt toast sent by two ladies to congratulate the Queen on her engagement. They burnt the toast because they were so excited!

A cinema, 500 tins of pineapple and two turkeys given to her as wedding gifts.

A model of Windsor Castle made out of chocolate.

A sloth, two jaguars, two giant tortoises and an elephant called Jumbo! They all lived at London Zoo.

ZOO

The Queen even has a part of Antarctica named after her – Queen Elizabeth Land – which is twice the size of the UK. I wonder if the penguins want to swap houses…

QUEEN ELIZABETH LAND

Jewels and fashion

The Queen does not own the Crown Jewels, but she gets to WEAR them!

The Crown Jewels are a very old and special collection of objects used by the royal family. It includes beautiful crowns such as St Edward's Crown, the one the Queen wore at her coronation. There are also huge swords and the Sovereign's Orb – a gold ball covered with precious stones and pearls. Many of these jewels came from countries that were part of the Empire, such as India and South Africa.

St Edward's Crown

Over 300 years ago, the Crown Jewels were stolen from the **TOWER OF LONDON** where they are kept. A man named Thomas Blood hammered one of the crowns with a mallet to make it easier to escape with, but he was caught and the crown was repaired!

St Edward's Crown is very heavy, and the Queen practised for her coronation by walking around balancing bags of *SUGAR* on her head. She says it "weighs a tonne".

The Crown Jewels

During the **SECOND WORLD WAR**, the Crown Jewels were taken from the Tower and hidden in the basement of Windsor Castle.

The jewels were hidden under a secret trapdoor, and the biggest stones were taken out and hidden in a biscuit tin! Elizabeth and Margaret were living in the castle at the time, but they weren't allowed to play with the crowns.

The Queen always wears brightly coloured clothes and small hats. She once said "I can never wear beige as no one will know who I am!"

The Queen is also famous for always carrying a **BLACK HANDBAG**. Apparently, if she swaps her bag from one arm to the other, it is a sign that she wishes to be moved to talk to someone else. What the Queen keeps in her handbag is a mystery, but we do know she often carries fruit cake in case she gets hungry!

Corgis and horses

The Queen may have lovely palaces, jewels and clothes, but one of the things she loves most is ANIMALS, especially dogs and horses!

When she was four, the Queen was given her first **HORSE**, a Shetland pony called **PEGGY**, and was immediately horse-mad! Once, Elizabeth's governess found the princess with a horse harness on her bed pretending to ride around a park.

The Queen's daughter, Anne, and her granddaughter, Zara, love horses too. They have even been part of the Great British **OLYMPIC** team!

The Queen loves dogs – especially corgis! Her first corgi was **DOOKIE**, who her father bought for the family when Elizabeth was seven. When she was 18, she was given her own corgi, **SUSAN**.

The Queen even invented a new breed of dog when one of her corgis had a puppy with a dachshund owned by her sister, Margaret. They named it a **DORGI**!

The Queen's daughter-in-law Princess Diana called the corgis the Queen's "moving carpet". There were so many of them, they looked like a giant rug.

They sleep in dog baskets in a special corgi room, eat freshly cooked meat every day and it is said that they even get their own stockings at Christmas.

The Queen has had more than 30 corgis over the years. The most famous were named **WILLOW** and **HOLLY**. The corgis come to lunch, meetings and even special dinners. Have you found them in this book? There is at least one on every page!

Big events

Elizabeth's Diary: Keep Out!

Life as the Queen means a lot of events. Did you see me meet James Bond and jump out of the helicopter at the Olympic opening ceremony in **2012?** (It wasn't really me, it was a stunt double. But I did really meet Bond!)

I celebrated being queen for **60** years with my Diamond Jubilee. It was a four-day event, and there was a parade of beautiful boats on the River Thames. People said I looked like Queen Elizabeth I when she sailed down the river.

But one of my favourite memories is when I turned **80**, and I had a special party at the Palace for **2,000** children.

The palace grounds were decorated like scenes from children's books with a giant model of the BFG playing the piano.
We had a delicious picnic and played so many fun games, including one where the Harry Potter actors investigated the theft of my handbag with spells!

Birthdays are always such fun, and lucky for me, I get two every year! My real birthday is in April, but my official birthday is in June. This is when we celebrate with a Trooping of the Colour – a fanfare of marching soldiers, horses and musicians. In the 1700s, King George II had his birthday in November, but he thought everyone would get cold watching the Troop, so he decided to have an official birthday in the summer. The tradition has lasted ever since.

I'd better go – afternoon tea is ready.

Elizabeth x

The Queen and her people

The Queen thinks it is very important to talk to the people of her country.

During the **SECOND WORLD WAR**, many children were evacuated, which meant they had to leave their homes in the city to stay with families in the countryside where it was safer. To make them feel better, the Queen gave a speech over the radio when she was 14.

Every year the Queen makes a Christmas speech. Her first **CHRISTMAS** message was shown on TV in 1957. There were bad weather conditions and some listeners got crossed wires and heard a New York police officer say, "Joe, I'm gonna grab a quick coffee"! It is now always pre-recorded just in case.

DID THE QUEEN JUST TURN AMERICAN AND SAY SHE WAS GOING TO GET A COFFEE?

The Queen does a lot of charity work and hosts regular
GARDEN PARTIES. Every year over 30,000 people who have
helped the country are invited to the garden parties.
They put on their best suits and hats, and between them,
they eat 20,000 pieces of cake, 27,000 cups of tea and
20,000 sandwiches. Sounds delicious!

MAIL

MAIL

The Queen receives around 60,000 **LETTERS**
every year.

She sends special messages to people who
turn 100 years old and to couples who have
been married for 60 years. The oldest ever
British person was Charlotte Hughes – she
lived to 115! If you were going to write to
the Queen, what would you say?

The Queen's family

The QUEEN has four children, eight grandchildren and lots of great-grandchildren. She also has over 30 godchildren. Now that's a lot of birthdays to remember!

Two of the most famous royals are Prince William and Prince Harry. Their dad is Prince Charles and one day he will be king. He and his wife Camilla are very passionate about farming and saving our planet. His car is even powered by **WHITE WINE** instead of **PETROL**!

PRINCE WILLIAM will be king after Prince Charles, because he is the oldest son. Millions of people watched him marry his wife, **KATE**, in 2011 and admired her beautiful **WEDDING DRESS**! Crowds lined the streets, waving flags and applauding with delight when the newlyweds kissed on the balcony of Buckingham Palace.

Kate met William when they were studying at **UNIVERSITY**. Together they do lots of charity work and travel for royal visits. Kate also loves playing sport and taking photos. They have three children – George, Charlotte and Louis.

William and Harry's mother was **PRINCESS DIANA**, who died in 1997. She was known as "The People's Princess". She was loved for helping other people in need, such as children in countries affected by war, and she worked with many charities.

HARRY is William's younger brother. He was a soldier after school, and he said he liked being treated as a soldier, not a prince. He set up the **INVICTUS GAMES** for wounded and sick soldiers to compete in sports.

Harry is married to **MEGHAN**, an American activist. She has worked with lots of charities around the globe. Meghan campaigns for a world in which people are treated equally, no matter who they are or what colour skin they have. She often makes great **SPEECHES** to help build up confidence in young girls.

Harry and Meghan have two children. The family now lives in America.

The Queen and her legacy

Elizabeth II has had the longest reign of any living king or queen in the world. That means she's a record-breaker!

Elizabeth II has been queen for more than 65 years and almost a third of British people – that's more than 22 million people – have seen her or met her!

Queen Elizabeth II

Prince of Wales

Duke of Cambridge

After the Queen, Prince Charles will become king. Next in line are William and his children, then Harry and his family. Up until 2013, boys always became king, even if they had an older sister. But now it goes in age order, so Princess Charlotte would become queen before Prince Louis became king.

Master Archie Mountbatten-Windsor

Duke of Sussex

Prince Louis of Cambridge

Princess Charlotte of Cambridge

Prince George of Cambridge

To Queen Elizabeth II
Buckingham Palace
London
SW1A 1AA

To Queen Elizabeth II
Buckingham Palace
London
SW1A 1AA

The Queen's face is on our **STAMPS, BANK NOTES** and **COINS**. Many of us can't quite imagine Britain without her. Prime ministers have come and gone, trends have changed, but the Queen has always been there.

Our record-breaking queen

Queens of England, Scotland and the United Kingdom

There are many great women who ruled England, Scotland and the United Kingdom before Queen Elizabeth II. Here are just a few of them and their amazing stories...

Matilda. Born in 1102.

Matilda very nearly became Britain's first female **MONARCH**. She was the only living child of Henry I, and he wanted her to be queen. But when Henry died, Matilda's cousin, Stephen, rushed to England and seized the throne first. She invaded England and fought for the **CROWN**. Though she failed, her son, Henry, made peace with King Stephen and eventually became king after him.

Lady Jane Grey. Born in 1537.

Can you imagine being queen for only a week? Well, Lady Jane Grey was. When she was 15, she became **QUEEN** for just one week and two days. But then Mary, her distant cousin, pushed Jane off the throne and **IMPRISONED** her in the Tower of London. Eventually, Queen Mary I had Jane's head chopped off! Poor Jane.

Elizabeth I. Born in 1533.

Elizabeth I was Henry VIII's daughter and a very powerful and successful queen. She was extremely **CLEVER** and knew Latin when she was just three years old! She loved plays by the famous writer William Shakespeare and even watched his shows. Elizabeth said she had "the body of a weak and feeble woman but the heart and stomach of a king".

Mary Queen of Scots. Born in 1542.

Mary Queen of Scots became queen when she was just six days old. She grew up in France and came back to rule **SCOTLAND** at the age of 18. But men, including her husbands, were always trying to take away her power. She was forced to give up the throne and went to England. But her cousin, Queen Elizabeth I, put her in prison for nearly 20 years and then chopped off her head!

Her son, **JAMES**, became King of Scotland. When Elizabeth I died, he became King of England too.

Victoria. Born in 1819.

When Queen Victoria was born, the name Victoria was very unusual and many people thought it was not a good name for a queen!

Victoria married her cousin, Albert, and they had nine children together. She loved him very much and when he died, she dressed in black for the rest of her life.

Lots of things were **INVENTED** while Victoria was queen, including the telephone and the penny-farthing bicycle. New factories, railways and towns were also built, but life was very hard for the poor and those people living under the British Empire.

There are many great queens from across the world as well.

RANI OF JHANSI was born in India in 1828. As a young girl, she learned to read and write, and trained in martial arts, horse riding and sword fighting! In the 1850s she fought against the British. Rani married a prince known as a maharaja. After his death, the army attacked her town. She trained her own army and fought back! She died in battle and is remembered as a *FIERCE* leader.

YAA ASANTEWAA was born around 1840 and was the Queen of the Ashanti in West Africa. The British were trying to gain control of the area, and in 1900 the King was sent away. The British said the country was theirs, but Yaa Asantewaa fought back! This strong and *FEARLESS* leader was eventually captured and sent to the Seychelles off the coast of East Africa.

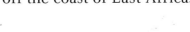

Our Queen Elizabeth

There have been lots of queens in history, but Elizabeth has been on the British throne longer than any of them.

Our Queen Elizabeth is very special. Since her coronation in 1953, she has put her duty to the crown first and has had a life that she could never have imagined. During her lifetime, she has seen the Second World War, the first Moon landing, the births of great-grandchildren and the world change dramatically. And through all of this, she has proved that women are great at being monarchs.

Elizabeth II has been a central presence at the heart of the United Kingdom and Commonwealth for over six decades, travelling around the country and around the world (sometimes with her beloved corgis!), meeting prime ministers and opening Parliament.

Hooray for the Queen!

For my lovely mum Veronica, with love – H.S.

First published in Great Britain in 2021
by Wren & Rook

Text copyright © Kate Williams, 2021
Illustrations copyright © Helen Shoesmith, 2021

The right of Kate Williams and Helen Shoesmith to be identified as author and illustrator respectively of this work has been asserted by them in accordance with the Copyright, Designs and Patents Act 1988.

Hardback ISBN: 978 1 5263 6329 9
Paperback ISBN: 978 1 5263 6331 2
E-book ISBN: 978 1 5263 6330 5
10 9 8 7 6 5 4 3 2 1

FSC
MIX
Paper from responsible sources
www.fsc.org
FSC® C104740

Wren & Rook
An imprint of
Hachette Children's Group
Part of Hodder & Stoughton
Carmelite House
50 Victoria Embankment
London EC4Y 0DZ

An Hachette UK Company
www.hachette.co.uk
www.hachettechildrens.co.uk

Managing Editor: Liza Wilde
Senior Commissioning Editor: Laura Horsley
Art Director: Laura Hambleton
Senior Designer: Sophie Gordon
Senior Editor: Sadie Smith

Printed in China